The Wife Who Submits

Operating In The Esther Spirit—A Guide For Wives And Wives-To-Be

Tavia S. Forrest

ISBN: 978-1-958404-14-0 (paperback)

Printed in the United States of America

Scripture quotations marked KJV are from the Holy Bible, King James Version (Authorized Version). First published in 1611. Quoted from the KJV Classic Reference Bible, Copyright 1983, by The Zondervan Corporation.

Scripture quotations marked (NIV) are taken from the Holy Bible, New International Version®, NIV®. Copyright © 1973, 1978, 1984 by Biblica, Inc.™ Used by permission of Zondervan. All rights reserved worldwide.

Scripture quotations marked (NLT) are taken from the Holy Bible, New Living Translation, copyright © 1996, 2004, 2007 by Tyndale House Foundation. Used by permission of Tyndale House Publishers, Inc., Carol Stream, Illinois 60188. All rights reserved.

Scripture quotations marked "NKJV" are taken from the New King James Version. Copyright © 1982 by Thomas Nelson, Inc. Used by

About marriage.
Rebellion is despised.
Submission attracts favor.

Dedication

To Edavia, my Sweetgirl, the fruit of my womb, my female child. I started writing this book before you were conceived,
and completed writing when you were eleven months old indeed.

I prayed for a boy child, but God blessed me with you,
And you fill my heart with so much joy; pink instead of blue.

I struggled with submission because of the hard things that I experienced,
But I vowed a life for you filled with joy, peace, and happy events.

May you never struggle with the things I did; I declare ancestral curses broken from you,
Because old things have passed away and behold all things have become new.

May you obtain grace to be obedient to the Word of God,
And experience all things beautiful with a life free from being sad.

I speak into your destiny, may your husband have a heart after God,

Just like the man who married me, your Holy Ghost-filled dad.

I love you, my Sweetgirl, I declare your future is blessed. As you obey the Word of God, He will do the rest.

Acknowledgments

Thanksgiving first goes out to Jesus Christ, my Lord and Savior, the Author and Finisher of my faith in whom I live, move, and have my being.

I thank God for this precious revelation from the book of Esther and for authorizing me, by His Spirit, to write this book. I didn't think I was the best-suited person to write this, but God showed me that He doesn't need my resume nor experience to qualify me for a task, so I yielded and thank Him for using me for this cause.

I thank my husband, Elder Forrest, for his never-ending support in my endeavors, and his love, patience, compassion, and encouragement to fulfill my assignments. Thank you, love, and God bless you.

To the two contributors to this book, Prophetesses R.J.S. and M.R.L. thank you for saying yes to the request, fulfilling the mandate, and sharing your experiences and wisdom concerning this titled book based on your many years in marriage. Lives will be touched for good.

To my Sweetgirl, Edavia, you are such a blessing, indeed a bundle of joy and my motivation to push so that in life you will know that giving up is not an option and obedience to God is better than sacrifice. Follow me as I follow Christ. As a female child of mine, I pray that this book will impact your life as it will many women around the world in appropriating the Word and order of God. Thank you for allowing mommy time to write. I love you.

Lastly, to you who are reading this book, may you or someone you know be positively and greatly impacted, and may the "God of all grace, who hath called us unto his eternal glory by Christ Jesus, after that ye have suffered a while, make you perfect, stablish, strengthen, settle you" (1 Peter 5:10) in this area of your union and marriage, in Jesus' name.

Thank you!

Table of Contents

Introduction
The Marriage Revelation

started writing this book in November 2020. I had been married for one year and eight months. My husband is a very peaceful man and expresses humility at its best. I think he has a special grace on him, but, of course, like all couples, we do not see eye to eye on everything, but we sincerely love each other. A friend of mine once said, "We don't always see eye to eye but always heart to heart."

With the "not always eye to eye" part, sometimes I found myself responding to my husband in a very distasteful way to a statement he would make or a question he would ask, if I was not in agreement with it. I even found myself from time to time speaking over him when he was speaking or belittling what he said. I noticed that each time it happened, he would put his foot down and set me straight, but I also realized that he would withdraw himself. He would avoid speaking for a little while, and when he did speak, it was but a few words. I really hated that, but there was this domineering, forceful spirit that operated in my life that I just could not understand. When those moments came, after my expression or response, I would feel so disgusted with myself to the point where I felt like I wanted to rip my skin off my body. I identified that it was a spirit, and I knew I didn't want it to be a part of me. I would get broken, repent, cry to the Lord and ask for help. I also prayed warfare prayers against that spirit because I identified what it was, and I knew it was not of God. I would go to my husband and repent as well because there are things we do at times, and it is not enough to repent to God alone; we must repent to those we have hurt and sinned against.

In my quiet time, the Holy Spirit would arrest my heart and convict me, reminding me that my husband is the man and he is the head that God has placed over me. The Holy Spirit showed me that I had an issue with "submission" and that needed to be dealt with.

I acknowledged this, but it was a battle. I never ceased to pray and declare that spirit be broken from my life. The Holy Spirit indeed reminds us of all things. He reminded me that growing up, my biological father wasn't around, and I felt angry about that. In addition, I witnessed fighting with my mother and stepfather, and my little brother got hurt in the process one day. (My brother has now passed, but it was not due to those fights. May his soul rest in peace).

My mother is small in stature. I have seen my stepdad abuse that fact. Many things went through my head, and I knew I would never allow a man to physically hurt me or otherwise for that matter. In addition to that, I frequently witnessed how my grandmother communicated with her husband, my grandfather, with disregard and contempt. However, little did I know that that was a seed being planted in my life, a seed that became a plant that needed to be uprooted; not physically uprooted with hands and feet but with Holy Ghost and with Fire.

The scripture says in 2 Corinthians 10:4 *"For the weapons of our warfare are not carnal, but mighty through God to the pulling down of strong holds."* The NIV says *"The weapons we fight with are not the weapons of the world. On the contrary, they have divine power to demolish*

15

strongholds." Whenever my grandma communicated in such a demeaning way to my grandpa, it would hurt me to the core. I did not understand the Bible then or even know the Word of God, but I knew in my heart that something was clearly wrong with that picture, and it went on for as long as they were alive. My older relatives would tell me that it was like that even before I was born.

The Lord brought me to a place and revealed to me that that is how most of the women in my family are; domineering, forceful, and must have the last say. I made up my mind and told God that I refused to treat my husband in that manner, and that spirit had to be broken from my life. I fasted and prayed even more radical prayers, tearing down this spirit of rebellion and being broken before the Lord. I was desperate for His help and asked for mercy. It was like a track and field relay event. My grandma ran the first leg, and the women in my family received the baton, running the same race of rebellion, then handing the baton over to their female children. But, I said, "NOT ME! In the name of Jesus Christ, I am disqualified from that race, and I will not carry that baton of rebellion."

Whatever we ask God for, not asking amiss, He will surely do. So, the Lord had me meditate on the Word more concerning marriage and submission of a wife to her husband. I took intentional steps. I watched videos and marriage sessions that dealt with these areas in-depth, and my bishop at the time, Courtney McLean, from Worship and Faith International Fellowship (WAFIF) in Jamaica, made it his life's mission to encourage the wives and husbands in their roles and would frequently put on this session called *'LETS REASON TOGETHER'* for couples and, oh, what a blessing those sessions were. I pushed because I was desperate to live a life that pleases God in every area. I made up my mind that the spirit of rebellion would not have dominion over me or my marriage and it would not be transferred to my children. I desired to not only be a hearer of the Word but a doer also, and to God be the glory, I progressed daily in being better.

Chapter One
The 'Esther' Revelation

In November 2020, Bishop Courtney McLean called the church to a 50-day Jubilee prayer. We came together at five each morning to seek the Lord, to wait in His presence, and have Him strip us of the things and ways that were not of God and fill us as to be more like Him. During regular church service within that time, Bishop was on the theme *'Faith to Destroy Foundational Wickedness/Iniquity.'* As he ministered and taught the church, the Lord started to open my eyes to the knowledge that the spirit of rebellion was a spirit coming from my ancestors, my generation, and that the foundation of it had to be dealt with and destroyed. It had to be rooted up, lest it continues to grow stronger and affect other females and marriages to come in my family.

One morning, as I quieted my heart before the Lord and yielded to the Holy Spirit, I clearly heard the word "**Esther.**" The first thing that came to my mind was the Book of Esther in the Bible, and I heard it repeatedly, even while driving. I thought to myself "My goodness, the Lord wants me to go on the Esther fast (which the book of Esther is known for to many persons), and I am currently taking antibiotics, which means I would have to eat." So, because of this thought, I procrastinated in reading it. The Holy Spirit kept reminding me that I still had not yet read the book of Esther. So, one night before I went to bed, I decided enough was enough and I said, "Lord, what do You want me to see?" I prayed my usual Psalm 119:18 request before I read the scripture, "Open my eyes, oh Lord, that I may behold wondrous things in Thy law."

As I started to read chapter one, the Lord opened my eyes to a brand-new revelation in the book of Esther. I had read it quite a few times before, but I never saw the revelation that the Lord gave me that night.

The Lord revealed the book of Esther to me as a book of submission. It highlighted the disobedience of a rebellious wife, Queen Vashti, and the consequences as a result of her losing everything, and compared it to the obedience and humility of Queen Esther, who instead of being rebellious, sought the Lord to obtain favor from her husband, the king.

For those of you who are already married and fall short in this area, this is vital to the success of your union and joy. For those of you engaged or aspiring to be married one day, take heed, pray, fast, and cry to the Lord for mercy and help in this area. This area of submission is an area the devil fights the most because being rebellious does not line up with the order of God, but being humble and meek springs forth joy and peace in a marriage. A rebellious spirit is one we should have no acquaintance with because the Bible says in 1 Samuel 15:23 *"rebellion (the opposite of submission) is as sinful as witchcraft..."* This is an area that many women are struggling with. Some have identified it and are praying about it; some are wondering why they operate in that way when they don't want to, and some don't even realize that they are operating in that spirit, so they think it is who they are, but this is not so. It is not normal, it is a spirit, and one that must be dealt with by force, fire, and power in Jesus' name.

21

Allow me to define what the word '*submission*' means for those who claim that submission is for weak women. To be submissive means to be humble, meek, loyal, and honorable. To operate in submission as a wife towards your husband means you are a very powerful woman, as this humility and meekness will cause favor to be extended to you from your husband in ways you could not imagine. It is not because of the man's will but because it is the order of God and His promises that once you obey His Word, there is great reward. Submission is not by force but by humbling yourself to honor God and those He has set as head over us. For example, submitting yourself to carrying out a task your pastor has requested of you without complaining, rebelling, or being disobedient because you don't feel like it or don't want to.

The Lord God Almighty gave me this revelation, and immediately I was led to put the revelation in writing. At first, I thought, "Why would GOD ask me or choose little old me to write any book on such a topic as submission?" I was not married for very long, so why not use someone who has mastered the art and has been married for many years? I thought to myself, "I have no experience in this area and, as a matter of fact, I am seeking help from Him to be better in this area, so why me?" But then He caused me to remember Jeremiah who was only a boy when He gave him an instruction, and Jeremiah's response was:

"O Sovereign Lord," I said, "I can't speak for you! I'm too young! The Lord replied, "Don't say, 'I'm too young,' for

you must go wherever I send you and say whatever I tell you. And don't be afraid of the people, for I will be with you and will protect you. I, the Lord, have spoken!" - Jeremiah 1:6-8 (NLT).

So, after this, I developed courage and asked the Lord for grace. I believe that whatever the Lord reveals, He reveals to heal.

Watch how Queen Esther receives favor from the king, her husband, by first seeking God's face and her attitude of humility and meekness, not by force or rudeness or rebellion. Please open your heart as you read and allow the Spirit of the living God to minister to your heart as He moves through the book of Esther to address the issue of submission, to change and fix that area in your marriage that you fall short in, and may the peace of God that passes all understanding guard your heart and mind through Christ Jesus. AMEN.

Chapter Two
The Rebellious Queen
(Vashti's Spirit - The Spirit That Leads To Separation)

*K*ing Ahasuerus (Xerxes) had the finest of things and liked displaying them, from the riches of his kingdom and the splendor of his majesty, to even his wife, Queen Vashti. The name Vashti means lovely, a very beautiful woman. According to the Bible and the king's request to show her off, Vashti embodied the meaning of her name in appearance; very beautiful. The king, her husband, requested her to display her beauty before all the people, even the king's officials. The king sent seven men to bring Queen Vashti before him. I asked myself, "Why did the king send seven men to bring one woman to him? Is it that she had a tendency to be violent and rebellious? Why could he not only send one to convey the message to her?" The Bible states that Queen Vashti refused to come at the king's command, which was delivered to her by the seven men, so the king became extremely angry and burned with rage.

Upon the king's request, his advisor advised him that he had to 'put his foot down' and rectify this form of disobedience and rebellion coming from his wife, the Queen. Otherwise, there would be an outbreak and great contempt coming from all the women. If he did not address it from that point of being a seed, all the other women would carry on that trend of being rebellious.

"Before this day is out, the wives of all the king's nobles throughout Persia and Media will hear what the queen did and will start treating their husbands the same way. There will be no end to their contempt and anger." (Esther 1:18 - NLT). This means all the women would begin to treat their

husbands in the same rebellious way, and their female children would come and adapt the same principles and posture towards their husbands. This would create what is called a generational curse. The advisor then suggested to the king that Vashti cease being queen, making an example out of her as to what the consequences of rebellion and disobedience to one's husband would be and that he finds someone more worthy to be called his wife and queen. By this, I believe the advisor meant someone more submissive, someone who knows how to give respect and honor to her husband irrespective of the place, condition, state he is in or the level he is at.

This statement made by the king's official advisor indicated that Vashti not only disrespected her husband, the king, but also disrespected all the men and their homes. The fact that Vashti was the queen meant that the wives or women of those men would see it as right or an accepted standard to disobey their own husbands, for they would say the queen did it and no consequences were attached, so we can do it too.

To make another point about Queen Vashti's disobedience, the king summoned her presence to his banquet, and the Bible said she was having her own separate banquet for the women in the palace. Hence, this obviously indicated that not only did she refuse and disrespect and disobey the king at his request in the presence of the seven men, but she did it in the presence of all the other women in the palace as well. Her actions and response showed that Queen Vashti, a wife, dishonored and disrespected her husband, the king. Hence, when the men reported back to the king, he became angry.

The king's anger and rage due to Vashti's rejection, and based on the advice given by his advisors, signifies that beauty does not and will never replace the principle of a wife being submissive, meek, and showing honor to her husband, who is the head, according to scriptures.

Sure, there are many women/wives now who believe that because of their beauty and 'goodly appearance' or physical attributes, business status, and job position that it should be enough and that submission is not necessary. Outside of being beautiful or not, a corporate female guru or not, the Word of God commands us to be submissive and show honor to our husbands. It does not even matter if we have more education than him or earn more than him; the order of God still stands. The husband is the head, saved or unsaved. If you are saved, and he is not, your humility and meekness added to seeking God may just save him. Therefore, as wives, it is crucial that we understand our positions in God's order.

If you wear the cap of a CEO at work and rule over or supervise other persons, you must be able to take that cap off at the end of your workday and put on the cap of a submissive wife. If you can identify an aggressive spirit towards your husband, disobedient and rebellious and not submissive, it is the spirit of rebellion that has entered your life somehow which needs to be broken. If this is not dealt with, then there is no guarantee that the marriage will survive because whether a woman is beautiful on the outside or not, once that woman is forceful, aggressive, and domineering, that is all the husband will see and not the physical beauty. As in the book of Esther, when the men delivered Queen Vashti's response to the king, he remembered nothing about her beauty that he wanted to show off, but only remembered how disobedient and disrespectful she was and how she made him feel small in the presence of everyone.

Obviously, the king liked showing off everything good that he had, including his beautiful queen, and because Queen Vashti was such a beautiful woman, I believe that if she was being the support God created us to be to our husbands, that the king would not have need to send for her in the first place. However, she chose to have her own separate banquet with all the other women in the province, observing her refusal to her husband, the king, and rebellion was displayed for all to see.

The Bible did not state how long the king and Queen Vashti were married, but the Lord had me thinking about what else she was denying her husband. If she openly dishonored the king in public, what else took place behind their closed chambers when there were no guests? What else could she be denying him as a wife? I believe Queen Vashti denied him intimacy and sex too, which is very important to a man. Yes, I know in those days the kings had their concubines whom they could lay with whenever, but I am specifically speaking of the role of a wife and the area of submission that the Lord revealed to me in the book of Esther. I believe Vashti did what she wanted when she wanted without addressing the king, spoke to him with aggression and pride instead of humility, and showed him no honor. If this was not the case, why would he need to send seven men to convey a message to one woman? I believe that behind closed doors, this act of rebellion was always displayed by Queen Vashti. It is not possible that she was always a wife of submission and humility, and then suddenly, on a night when the king, her husband, was entertaining guests that she chose to openly reject him. This was who she was, maybe coming down from her lineage of forefathers and ancestors. I believe most of her rebelliousness happened in private, and he did not dare to discuss or share with anyone. After all, he was the king and would not want to lose the respect of the people. However, because this act of refusal and dishonor displayed by his wife, Queen Vashti, was done openly, he had no choice but to put an end to it, especially when the advice of the advisor sounded so logical to him. Hence, the decree was sent out and her position as queen was taken away.

Chapter Three
He Was Created With An Ego

The Lord showed me that many wives are operating and displaying this character of dishonor and displaying actions of rebellion toward their husbands, and it must stop now. God created men to lead, not in aggression or pride, but in humility and Godly authority. The man is the head of his wife and household; Christ is the head of the man, and God is the head of Christ. Any actions or anything contrary to this order is a sin against the Lord.

The Bible says wives must submit (honor, respect) their husbands, and husbands should love their wives as Christ loves the church (see Ephesians 5:22-25). God put a DNA in men (male species) with a need to be respected and honored, so if we, as wives, tear them down with our words, operate in rebellion, or disrespect them, it is as if something is literally being pulled from them that shuts them down, something that causes them not to operate and be functional in his role as the head. God created men with an ego, an ego that needs to be nurtured with respect. However, this kind of ego was not meant to be hardcore and prideful, but it naturally causes him to have that need and be in that position to take care of his family. If you meet a man who does not display this, then they have not reached that level of maturity, and that ego God created him with is not yet activated. Have you ever noticed how irresponsible some men are until they become a father? He then starts to be responsible with a need of wanting to provide for that child. Notice I said "Some men." The point is, something activated his God-given ego.

Husbands want their wives to respect them and rely on them, and that form of respect is not bowing down physically, but it is a form of meekness in your attitude—it is that Esther spirit. Had Vashti displayed that form of meekness towards her husband, the king, history would have been rewritten. She would have remained queen, and maybe we would not have even heard of Esther.

Wives want to feel secured and cherished, but you will never experience that feeling from your husband if you continue to display a "Vashti spirit"; rebellious and mean. Two things go hand in hand: a wife's submission and a husband's love. It is just the order of God. Therefore, by submitting to your husband, you fulfill his need to encourage him to take care of yours too. The result of fulfilled needs between a husband and wife ensures a long and happy marriage. This submission in marriage is a spirit of respect that a wife has toward her husband. It is an attitude intended to help her and her husband to live a more contented and peaceful life together. Isn't that what you want and desire for your union?

Chapter Four
I'm Busy

I know many women these days, like myself, are career-oriented and very independent, but when it comes to your marriage, shake off that spirit of independence and ask the Lord to put on the spirit of meekness on you. Learn to become a sweet, soft-spoken, tender baby to your husband in your actions and when you speak to him. Wives, I assure you by doing this, he will move mountains for you. Let him feel strengthened and masculine; give him that power and Godly place of protection over you.

Many wives have become so modernized and busy with being career-oriented to the point where they do not have the time to prepare a home-cooked meal for their family. The modernized way of being career-oriented, making your own money, and sometimes earning more than the man, can cause you to operate and behave as if you don't need your husband. You are making more money so you can do whatever you want, whenever you want. Like Vashti, you may say or think "My beauty is so exquisite, it doesn't matter what I do. He will not want to give me up." But this is a dishonor to your husband.

Many wives, because they are "not in the mood," deny their husbands intimacy and sex and will only give in when they feel like it, but God says this is a dishonor to your husband according to:

1 Corinthians 7:4 - For the wife does not have authority over her own body, but the husband does. Likewise, the husband does not have authority over his own body, but the wife does. (ESV).

May I say right now that this is the reason many females do not want to be saved and become kingdom women because there are statutes and precepts to obey that they are not willing to yield to. I assure you, being born again or not, the Word of God <u>still stands,</u> and we will have to give an answer to Him on the day of judgment.

Many wives speak over their husbands, ignore what they say, and rebel, but God says this is a dishonor to your husbands.

Many wives are contentious and quarrelsome, picking a fight with their husbands at every chance, which then causes him to withdraw himself and cringe going home after work, but God says this is a dishonor. The Bible says *"It is better to live in a corner of the housetop than in a house shared with a quarrelsome wife." (Proverbs 21:9 – ESV).*

Many wives disrespect their husbands by the aggressive way they respond, but God says this is a dishonor. The Bible says *" ...and let the wife see that she respects her husband." (Ephesians 5:33b – ESV).*

Many wives desire every care and things of the world and, as a result, ignore her husband's needs, but God says this is a dishonor to your husband. The Bible says *"Your desire shall be contrary to your husband, and he shall rule over you." (Genesis 3:16b – ESV).*

Many wives wear the cap of a CEO, manager, or supervisor at work, and when they arrive home, they still keep on the

37

hat of being the head of their firm and treat their husbands as they treat and dictate to their staff. God says this is a dishonor, for the Bible says *"But I want you to understand that the head of every man is Christ, the head of a wife is her husband, and the head of Christ is God." (1 Corinthians 11:3 – ESV).*

Many wives are naked because they are not clothe with the spirit of humility, humbling themselves before the husband God placed over them, but God says this is a dishonor to your husbands. The Bible says *"as Sarah obeyed Abraham, calling him lord." (1 Peter 3:6a – ESV).*

Many wives, because of their display of rebellion and public disrespect to their husbands with others watching, cause those who desire marriage to be bitter against it and the image that God created marriage to be. God says this is a dishonor. The Bible says *"to be self-controlled, pure, working at home, kind, and submissive to their own husbands, that the word of God may not be reviled." (Titus 2:5 – ESV).*

Chapter Five
Compromise And Agree To Disagree

When we were little children, we desired and could not wait to get older because we were of the mindset that when we get older, we are grown and can do as we feel, when we feel and how we feel without the consent or agreement of others. This may be true in some cases, but when it comes to marriage, it is completely the opposite.

In Matthew 19:6, Jesus says the husband and wife are no longer two but <u>one</u>. This means you are no longer your own, doing what you want to do when you want to do it without considering anyone, but you have become one with your partner. It is important and necessary for both of you to be in agreement on whatever you have decided to do.

As a wife, when preparing a meal, you will have to consider your husband whether he eats that particular meat or not. You want to ensure that your husband will be able to partake in the meal you are preparing. Hence, it is no longer "I will cook what I want," but it is now "What will we have for dinner tonight?"

I remember when my status was "single," and my friends would call me for a weekend getaway and a night out. I would make my own decision whether I wanted to go or not. Now being married, when the call to go have a drink comes up by a friend, I have to *suggest* it to my husband and ensure he is okay with it and in agreement with me going. Notice, I did not say "I will have to *tell* my husband" but rather *suggest* it to my husband. Saying "*I will tell* my husband that I'm going," suggest that I already made my mind up to go whether he agrees or not. Using the word 'suggest' is also for you to understand that it is a civil relationship, not a prisoner and guard relationship or union. I assure you, women, this is not weakness, this is <u>strength!</u> I have become one with him. Being married doesn't mean you have gone back to being a child, but it demonstrates meekness and humility, which creates peace, joy, and a sense of respect. Disagreement will come because you will not agree on everything all the time; however, disagreeing doesn't mean being harsh, aggressive, and disrespectful, but agreeing to disagree. Also—this is very important—if you know with all your heart that your husband is wrong, pray to the Lord about it and ask the Lord to show him the right and allow him to understand your point of view. I tell you this from experience. As a matter of fact, that is what the Lord expects you to do and not to be rebellious and speak down to your husband. After all, God placed Him as head over you, so it is the same God you have to go to in order to fix the situation. If you know your husband is wrong about a particular situation, keep your position of humility and meekness, God will do the rest. The spirit of meekness and humility is enough to win him over and cause him to think about what he said to you or what he did wrong.

1 Peter 3:1 says *"Likewise, ye wives, be in subjection to your own husbands; that, if any obey not the word, they also may without the word be won by the conversation of the wives."*

If you demonstrate being aggressive, rebellious, and revengeful, that is all he will think about and even forget that he did wrong. This kind of attitude angers not only a husband but any man. You see, God created men with a certain ego that makes them feel masculine; therefore, any conversation that tampers with that ego automatically puts them in a position of anger; some men shut down. Queen Vashti was one such wife who was disobedient and rebellious; she tampered with the king's ego. He wanted to show off his wife, but she belittled him and disobeyed him in open public. The king quickly forgot how beautiful she was, and wrath took over. She tampered with his ego as a man and as a king. This tells me that humility and meekness are more beautiful than any physical appearance.

Physical appearance fades away after a while but having a spirit of meekness and humility stays with you until death. It never fades, never wears out. Some persons were born naturally humble, while others started to operate in that spirit over time, whether it is a life situation that caused it or they sought God for it. As wives, we must operate in this spirit and be submissive to our husbands as Jesus commands. If you were not naturally born a humble and meek person, and you realize that is your struggle, start seeking God to give you that spirit. I encourage you to go into serious prayer and fasting. If you want your marriage to last and glorify God, you must do this because a rebellious and brass, contentious spirit will not win your husband over.

Many men cringe when it is time to go home. They find excuses to hang out with a friend and start making the liquor store or bar their one-stop after work because they know the rebellious and verbally abusive wife they have to go home to. Isn't that just sad? Very sad, if you asked me. The Bible says in Proverbs 25:24 *"It is better to dwell in a corner of a housetop, than in a house shared with a contentious woman."* *(NKJV)*. The Bible also states *"A continual dripping on a very rainy day and a contentious woman are alike;"* (Proverbs 27:15 - NKJV). Proverbs 27:16 says *"Restraining her is like restraining the wind or grasping oil with the hand."* *(NIV)*.

As a wife, having a spirit of meekness and humility is key in marriage. In 1 Peter 3:7, the Bible says the husband should give honor unto the wife as unto the weaker vessel. If the wife is operating as a man, then this makes it hard for the husband to see her as the weaker vessel, so we have our part to play in order for the Word of God to manifest. I am sure the king did not see Vashti as the weaker vessel as she operated in this fashion of disobedience and rebellion toward her husband.

43

Chapter Six
Vashti vs. Queen Esther

*L*et us compare Vashti's attitude to Queen Esther's. Now, remember, the king remarries, and a young lady called Esther became his wife. From reading the scriptures, you see that Esther was a completely opposite character to Vashti. In Esther 4, Mordecai (Esther's uncle) wanted her to go to the king to plead on the Jews' behalf because their life was threatened. In Esther 4:11, this is what Esther sent to tell him: *"All the king's servants, and the people of the king's provinces, do know, that whosoever, whether man or women, shall come unto the king into the inner court, who is not called, there is one law of his to put him to death, except such to whom the king shall hold out the golden scepter, that he may live: but I have not been called to come in unto the king these thirty days." (KJV)*.

Though she had the position of being the queen, she was submissive to his authority and the rules he had for anyone coming to see him without being called. In Esther 4:16, Queen Esther decided that she would go to the king and said to herself, *"If I perish, I perish."* Note what Esther did before she made that statement; she went on a fast. She sought God's face, that He would release grace upon her to get favor from the king when she entered his chamber without being called. Most certainly she received favor when she entered the king's chamber.

Esther's way of going about the situation demonstrated grace, meekness, and humility. God honored her for that and granted her favor. Are you demonstrating the 'ESTHER' spirit towards your husband and in your marriage so that you may win your husband over with God's favor? Are you operating in submission? If the answer is 'no,' start seeking God now to help you because without it, you are headed for a fall, a separation, or unease in your union.

Become a child again in the spirit of humility. Demonstrate meekness. Be submissive.

Chapter Seven
Submission Attracts Favor

W e are women of purpose and power. Most of us don't even know the power we carry or that God has bestowed upon us. Therefore, it is important that we fellowship with God and have a relationship with Him. This constant fellowship and relationship with Him, by His Spirit, will cause you to learn His will and obey His Word.

Many women today are living ungodly lives. They have rebelled against God's plans and the commands He has set for us to follow. I am stating this fact because we cannot become all God intends for us as women of purpose and power unless we seek Him. You will never be that wife of submission and humility if you don't seek fellowship and a relationship with God. You will never receive the favor of God upon and in your life if you don't seek Him wholeheartedly. Notice what Esther did; she knew she was not supposed to enter her husband's (the king's) chamber unless she was called or summoned, so she went in prayer and fasting to seek the favor of God for this bold move, and indeed, God favored her. After the fast and she went to the king's chamber, instead of him being angered and wrath, he welcomed her with grace. Esther 5:2-3 states:

And it was so, when the king saw Esther the queen standing in the court, that she obtained favor in his sight: and the king held out to Esther the golden sceptre that was in his hand. So Esther drew near and touched the top of the sceptre. Then said the king unto her, What wilt thou, queen Esther? and what is thy request? it shall be even given thee to the half of the kingdom. (KJV).

WOW! What a fellowship! What a favor! The king was willing to give Queen Esther half of the kingdom, if that was her request. Fellowship with GOD truly creates grace for favor, and submission attracts favor. I assure you, by the knowledge of GOD, that the favor Esther obtained in his sight is due to her humility. Had Queen Esther demonstrated an attitude like Vashti, the results would have been completely different, and the history of this story would have been written differently.

Many times my husband and I disagree on some things, and I know I am right, but instead of tearing him down or becoming rebellious, I allow him to have the last say. I then ask the Lord to show him and let him understand my point of view and, of course, the covenant-keeping God never fails. To be honest, sometimes this is rather hard to do, but my husband would come back hours or days later saying something like "I thought about what you said, and you are right. I'm sorry. I understand what you were saying." Surely that is God. Remember, God created men with an ego, so only God can give Him that unction to admit his error and apologize.

Maybe you are saying, "Oh, good for you. No matter what, my husband never apologizes when he does anything or is in the wrong." Take a step back and see how you contributed to this stubbornness of his. Did you tear him down with some words that cut deeper than a knife? Are you normally rebellious? Are you the type of person who does things when you want or how you want? Are you in fellowship with God so He can move on your behalf as He did for Esther? Are you praying for your husband that the Lord will change his heart and mind? Or are you a Queen Vashti? Look back, get a pen and paper, write down where you think you fall short, and go into prayer. God can do all things, and He is a God who honors marriages. In addition to that, He is a rewarder to them who diligently seek Him (see Hebrews 11:6). Marriage is created to be an honorable union, and as women, wives, wives-to-be, and aspiring wives, we have to fulfill our part with grace.

Maybe you are saying, "My husband is dishonoring our marriage. He is having an affair and I know it. I have been a good wife. How can I continue to honor him and be submissive to him?" My very hard but honest answer to you is, continue to honor him, continue to be humble even though you are hurting, continue to be submissive and, most of all, continue to stay in that fellowship with God. If you are not doing it, I suggest you start now.

Let me share someone's true testimony with you. There was a testimony made by this married couple, both saved Christians, but the wife had such a fellowship and strong relationship with the Lord. Her husband, however, was not so deep in Christ. He started to have an affair with another woman, and he would leave his wife and his matrimonial bed just to sleep out with the woman he was having the affair with. He would sleep at the lady's house where her family lived and give excuses to his wife, for example, work duty. His wife knew that he was being unfaithful. She knew he was having an affair, and she was hurt. One day he was about to leave home to go on his planned adulterous mission, and he took out the clothes he was going to wear and was about to put them on. She said to him, "You can't go like that. Let me iron your clothes." She ironed them really well, made his breakfast, and wished him a good day as he set out. While he was on his way to the woman's house, something came over him, and he started to think, "How can my wife still be so good to me and humble after all I'm doing to her?" The Lord began to move on his heart. He still continued his journey to the lady's house, and when he got there and went in, the lady said to him, "What are you doing here?"

He replied, "What do you mean? You know I always come on this night."

She said to him, "You can't stay. This is not going to work out."

Her mother came out and said to him, "Young man, go home to your wife." He left in shock because he did not understand the sudden change of heart towards him. On His way home, he cried like a baby, wondering how he could do such a thing to his wife, who has been nothing but good and faithful to him. When He got home and went inside, she was on her knees praying. He said, "I have something to tell you. I have not been faithful."

She said, "I know, but I know God would have to fight the battle for me."

He cried like a baby and repented to her. He said, "How could you know all this time and still do all you do without a murmur?"

She said, "That's the only way God would come through for me, if I obeyed Him by being humble and submissive, holding my position. It was hard." They got counseling. She is a pastor today, and he is a minister. What a submission! She operated in what I call the "Esther spirit." What a mighty and faithful God we serve.

It pays to be a submissive wife like Esther and not rebellious like Vashti. Stay in fellowship with God. Seek Him like Esther and be confident that He will do the rest. Submission truly attracts favor.

Proverbs 31:10-12 says – *"An excellent wife who can find? She is far more precious than jewels. The heart of her husband trusts in her, and he will have no lack of gain. She does him good, and not harm, all the days of her life."* *(ESV).*

Chapter Eight
Honor Him Above His Level of Education

Education has nothing to do with God's commands and His instruction to honor because God does not need our resume to qualify us.

After the king gave the advisors permission to proceed with their suggestion, they said, *"So if it pleases the king, we suggest that you issue a written decree, a law of the Persian and Medes that cannot be revoked. It should order that Queen Vashti be forever banished from the presence of King Xerxes and that the king should choose another queen more worthy than she." They then said, "When this decree is published throughout the king's vast empire, husbands everywhere, whatever their rank, will receive proper respect from their wives!" (Esther 1:19-20 – NLT).* In other words, husbands, irrespective of influence or education, ought to receive honor and respect from their wives.

Let this be a word to you; irrespective of your husband's level of education, whether he was a high school graduate or not, or whether he attended the most prestigious Ivey League educational institution or not, God has no regard for that. The scripture in Ephesians 5:22 says, *"Wives, submit yourselves unto your own husbands, as unto the Lord." (KJV).* It did not say submit to your husband according to his level of education. Once he is named "Your husband," submission is a command for wives, and anything outside of that is utter rebellion. Submission is not only towards your husband but towards God, as the scripture states *"....as unto the Lord."*

In the Kingdom, there are spiritual rules and laws that must be adhered to in order to experience certain grace. Therefore, you cannot treat your husband with disregard and contempt and then talk about honoring God. I assure you, God cannot receive honor from you in the spirit when in the natural you are rebellious.

The Bible says, *"...for whatever a man sows, that he will also reap." (Galatians 6:7)*. Vashti had sown seeds of rebellion and disregard, and her reward was reaping the anger of the king and his advisors who agreed to banish her from the kingdom and find another who was more worthy. Queen Esther, on the other hand, sowed seeds of humility and sought God for what she needed, and her reward was the grace of favor.

Chapter Nine
Seasoned Wives: A Contribution to Submission Based on Their Years of Marriage

I am sure that for persons who are married for many years, their experience and life together were not always a walk in the park. How could it be when the adversary fights us daily, especially for the things of God? I am certain that these couples who have been working the mill for these many years have faced trials and tribulations, with everyone's own issues and testimony being different.

God has brought me to a house, a church home, where I'm surrounded by women who have been married for many years, so I had the awesome privilege of speaking with two of whom I was led to speak to in regard to this topic of submission, how important it is to their union, and how it benefited them as they yielded to their own husbands. This was their response to the call.

Please note, I will use only initials for privacy reasons.

Submitted by Prophetess R.J.S.

When I got married forty-four years ago, things were different in the world and in the church. When I think of the word "submission" from a Christian wife's position, it, in this day and time, has become a distasteful word, maybe because it is misunderstood and/or the narrative the world has given it has a negative connotation.

The Word of God declares order and the position of the husband and wife. However, it takes the compliance of both for it to work according to His design. So, I speak to those who love and believe in the Lord, not to the world that has designed its own way of life.

What is submission in marriage? In definition, it is a spirit of respect a wife has toward her husband. It is an attitude intended to help her and her husband to live a more content and peaceful life together. It is also an act that is expressed mutually and voluntarily. It helps us to be less self-centered and allows us to consider the desires of others. It has nothing to do with being weak but allows us to be strong enough to open our hearts to others.

So, as the scripture in Ephesians 5:22 speaks to us as wives being submissive to our husbands, it is not short in its position for our husbands as well. Ephesians 5:25 is as powerful and instructive as it can be.

I am not aware if there is a wife who does not want and need to be loved, as Ephesians 5:25 declares. The thought of what Christ did and showed towards the church is exemplified by a husband towards his wife, which would be the highest pinnacle of love, which then rebounds to the willing respect and submission of a wife to her husband. From my perspective, this was and is the intent of a Godly union.

Submitted by Prophetess M.R.L.

I am from a dysfunctional background; there was fighting, arguing, and a great need for control between my mother, father, and, later, stepfather. There were fights typically late at night, which left us, my siblings and mother, tired and

61

exhausted. This dominated my childhood and adulthood until I left home to attend college.

When I met my husband, I was twenty-six years old and unprepared for a relationship. Getting over a previous relationship six months earlier, I was strong-willed and determined not to let my life be like my mother's. My husband did not stand a chance! We were so different in many ways; culturally, we were raised differently. He was older, I was younger; he lived at home, I was living with my oldest brother, essentially on my own. I was extremely independent because I grew up taking care of my siblings; he was more dependent because he was the son who returned from military duty and stayed home. The sense of control was my driving force when I said "I do" six months after we met.

God is perfect in all His ways! I could not have predicted the course of my life or God's intentions when He allowed me to marry my husband. Isaiah 55:8-9 sums it up nicely. What God destines for us is so different from what we plan for ourselves. My husband and I were newly saved when we said, "I do"—six months to be exact; therefore, our expectations were naïve and unrealistic at best. We were fighting all the time. I was not happy and was not acclimated to the idea of being accountable to another adult. I resisted releasing control of my life to my spouse and to God. It was frustrating and extremely troubling for me because I did not understand what I was doing. It appeared I was not getting this "marriage" thing right. I would go to the bathroom and cry out in prayer, tearful and fearful because I felt I had made a huge mistake!

I recall one particular day, I went to my husband's job to get something from him. While there, we got into an argument, and I began to be condescending and belittling. Of course, I did not realize that was what I was doing until the Lord stopped me in my tracks and asked, "Who gave you the ability to read and write? Who gave you the opportunity to go to college?" You see, I thought I was smarter and knew better than God; therefore, I was not willing to let my spouse be the head (see Ephesians 5:22-23). This would be one of many lessons in our journey—my journey—to learn my role and position in my marriage.

To say things went smoothly after that is an understatement. God is truly a good, good Father because the patience, longsuffering, and mercy He applied to my life during this time was only by the love of a Father. During this process, there was a lot I needed to learn about who I am and my place within my marriage. Submission was proving difficult to grasp. I wanted to please the Lord and be obedient, but I was struggling to trust Him with my life and trust my husband with my heart. One day I felt I could do it, and the next, I was saying and doing the wrong thing—there was so much I had to learn.

God is never without a plan for His children, and I can appreciate that. He knows the beginning to the end of all things, and I had to learn trusting and obeying Him is the most important part of submission. We are not always privy to what God has in store for us, but we can be assured of one thing, *"...all things work together for good to them that love God, to them who are the called according to His purpose."* *(Romans 8:28 – KJV).* I could not have scripted one of the most pivotal lessons of submission in 2010.

I graduated from college in 2009 and was seeking the Lord as to what my next steps would be. My main goal for going back to college was to be able to secure a good-paying job to live financially secure, but that was far from what happened. How could I not find a Job? With a degree in hand and for all countless applications submitted, I could not secure a job. Instead of a secular job, the Lord offered me a job working in the ministry as the Social Outreach Administrator. What?

This meant I would need to yield to my husband as the only provider, and I would have to trust him and God to be my caretaker. What a lesson!

The Lord was centering me positionally in my marriage, and with one stroke, He had me where He wanted me. Wow! It was not clear at first where this was going, but by now, I knew enough to say, "Okay, Lord, I'll trust You." What? Who was this person? This was the woman God had been after when I left my mother's home and said I would never depend on or allow a man to tell me what to do. God was doing a new thing in my life.

Yielding was the best decision I could have made because a divine shift was released in my life—and our lives; my husband and I would not be the same in the year of writing this (2022). We are thirty-three years married!

Final Word From The Author

A submissive wife is not a weak woman but rather a woman of strength and honor. It is not easy on our own, so we have to stay in the Word, that is, reading the Bible, meditating, and staying on our knees in prayer. The same knees you went on to ask God for your husband are the same knees you ought to go on and ask God for grace to obey His Word, and that your husband would also obey and fulfill his part as scripture declares in Ephesians 5:21-23:

"Submitting yourselves one to another in the fear of God. Wives, submit yourselves unto your own husbands, as unto the Lord. For the husband is the head of the wife, even as Christ is the head of the church: and he is the Savior of the body." (KJV).

The Bible says the husband is the head of the wife, so my charge to you is, if you are married to one who is operating out of the order of God, which makes submission for you difficult, your duty as a wife is still to submit while you are in prayer seeking the Lord for him to lead your home according to scripture. I know in this day and time, most women desire to go to college, have a business, job, etc., which is all good, but true success comes from and begins by us being obedient to the Word of God. Once we fulfill that first mandate, God makes everything beautiful because He is bound by His Word.

As a wife or wife-to-be, remember that submission is key. Submission is demonstrating meekness and humility towards your husband, and submission attracts favor.

Submission is the Esther Spirit: "If I perish, I perish," but first, seek God's face in all things.

Esther demonstrated complete submission to her husband, not because he was the king but because she understood that submission and prayer are the keys to activating God's favor toward her. No one was allowed to enter the king's chamber unless requested by Him, but Esther knew that men did not make themselves, but it was God, who is also able to move upon their hearts. The Bible said that the king *"...loved Esther above all the women, and she obtained grace and favor in his sight more than all the virgins;" (Esther 2:17a – KJV)*. Esther 5:2a says *"When the king saw Esther the Queen standing in the court, that she obtained favor in his sight..." (KJV)*. Esther conducted herself with much meekness and humility. Each time she went into the presence of the king, her husband, she obtained favor in his sight. The king said, *"Tell me what your request is, and it shall be given to you even if it's half of the kingdom" (Esther 5:3 paraphrased)*. Isn't submission powerful? Which wife would not want to experience such favor, where their husband would want to move mountains for them by all means? I sure do.

So, you see, the submissiveness of a wife is a strength and not a weakness. We ought to learn to agree to disagree and take the big things, and even the small ones, to prayer like Esther. I know so many persons who are experiencing challenges in their marriages. The devil is rampant, and he knows that if we are not obedient to God, there is room for him to work and cause mayhem. So, this is one of the main areas of a marriage that the enemy attacks.

2 Corinthians 2:11 says *"in order that Satan might not outwit us. For we are not unaware of his schemes." (NIV).*

All the entitlement we feel to all the promises and blessings that come along with belonging to the Lord, the condition of that is to be obedient to His Word. God has placed us over our children, and we want them to submit to us when we speak and be obedient to the rules we set in the house. At the same time we do not want to submit and be obedient to God's precepts and ways for our lives, and He is our Father. In John 2:5, Jesus' mother said to the servants, *"Do whatever He tells you" (NLT),* and by the servants' act of obedience, Jesus was able to turn water into wine.

Wives and wives-to-be, we ought to take Mary's counsel and do what God tells us to do because He is bound by His Word and can only change situations and move upon people's hearts, like our husbands, in favor of us, only if we move in obedience. Obedience is not pride; obedience is humility. We love it when our children say, "Yes, mom, I will do it," so we ought to say, "Yes, God, I will do it!"

We must change our heart's posture towards submission. Wives, fiancés, and aspiring wives, let us operate in the Esther spirit, which is the spirit of humility, meekness, obedience, and submission. Let us ask God daily to grant us the grace to be prayerful so we may experience contentment, love, and peace in our home and in our union.

Submission is a highly sought-after quality by the Lord. Being submissive tells God He can trust you and use you.

Esther, God is calling you!

About the Author

Tavia S. Forrest was born and raised in the parish of St. Catherine, between the communities of Spanish Town and Portmore, Jamaica. She is the second child born to her mother, whom she loves dearly. Tavia and her husband, Elder Edward Forrest, share a home in Bloomfield, Connecticut with their two children, Edavia, who is a product of their marriage and, Autumn, her stepdaughter.

Tavia is very passionate about her walk with Christ and pushes for more of Him daily. Due to migration from Jamaica to the United States, she is now a member of the Bibleway Temple Nation Church in Hartford, Connecticut, where she currently serves the Lord in the Youth and Cradle Ministry department. Tavia is vibrant, family-oriented, and a people-person. She firmly believes that if you connect your walk to God's Word, you will, without a doubt, experience the manifestation of His promises. Tavia is also the author of *"A Walk In The Word: Connecting Your Walk To The Word of God (Volume 1)."*

Her personal pillow Scripture is Psalm 16:8 - *"I have set the Lord always before me: because He is at my right hand, I shall not be moved." (KJV)*.

www.ingramcontent.com/pod-product-compliance
Lightning Source LLC
Chambersburg PA
CBHW070134100426
42744CB00009B/1833